"It's hard to connect with your child without first understanding where they are. As counselors and speakers at parenting events across the country, we spend a great deal of time teaching parents about development. To know *where* your child is—not just physically, but emotionally, socially, and spiritually, helps you to truly know and understand *who* your child is. And that understanding is the key to connecting. The Phase Guides give you the tools to do just that. Our wise friends Reggie and Kristen have put together an insightful, hopeful, practical, and literal year-by-year guide that will help you to understand and connect with your child at every age."

SISSY GOFF
M.ED., LPC-MHSP, DIRECTOR OF CHILD & ADOLESCENT COUNSELING AT DAYSTAR COUNSELING MINISTRIES IN NASHVILLE, TENNESSEE, SPEAKER AND AUTHOR OF ARE MY KIDS ON TRACK?

"These resources for parents are fantastically empowering, absolute in their simplicity, and completely doable in every way. The hard work that has gone into the Phase Project will echo through the next generation of children in powerful ways."

JENNIFER WALKER
RN BSN, AUTHOR AND FOUNDER OF MOMS ON CALL

"We all know where we want to end up in our parenting, but how to get there can seem like an unsolved mystery. Through the Phase Project series, Reggie Joiner and Kristen Ivy team up to help us out. The result is a resource that guides us through the different seasons of raising children, and provides a road map to parenting in such a way that we finish up with very few regrets."

SANDRA STANLEY
FOSTER CARE ADVOCATE, BLOGGER, WIFE TO ANDY STANLEY, MOTHER OF THREE

"Not only are the Phase Guides the most creative and well-thought-out guides to parenting I have ever encountered, these books are ESSENTIAL to my daily parenting. With a 13-year-old, 11-year-old, and 9-year-old at home, I am swimming in their wake of daily drama and delicacy. These books are a reminder to enjoy every second. Because it's just a phase."

CARLOS WHITTAKER
AUTHOR, SPEAKER, FATHER OF THREE

"As the founder of Minnie's Food Pantry, I see thousands of people each month with children who will benefit from the advice, guidance, and nuggets of information on how to celebrate and understand the phases of their child's life. Too often we feel like we're losing our mind when sweet little Johnny starts to change his behavior into a person we do not know. I can't wait to start implementing the principles of these books with my clients to remind them . . . it's just a phase."

CHERYL JACKSON
FOUNDER OF MINNIE'S FOOD PANTRY, AWARD-WINNING PHILANTHROPIST, AND GRANDMOTHER

"I began exploring this resource with my counselor hat on, thinking how valuable this will be for the many parents I spend time with in my office. I ended up taking my counselor hat off and putting on my parent hat. Then I kept thinking about friends who are teachers, coaches, youth pastors, and children's ministers, who would want this in their hands. What a valuable resource the Orange team has given us to better understand and care for the kids and adolescents we love. I look forward to sharing it broadly."

DAVID THOMAS
LMSW, DIRECTOR OF FAMILY COUNSELING, DAYSTAR COUNSELING MINISTRIES, SPEAKER AND AUTHOR OF ARE MY KIDS ON TRACK? AND WILD THINGS: THE ART OF NURTURING BOYS

"I have always wished someone would hand me a manual for parenting. Well, the Phase Guides are more than what I wished for. They guide, inspire, and challenge me as a parent—while giving me incredible insight into my children at each age and phase. Our family will be using these every year!"

COURTNEY DEFEO
AUTHOR OF IN THIS HOUSE, WE WILL GIGGLE, MOTHER OF TWO

"As I speak to high school students and their parents, I always wonder to myself: What would it have been like if they had better seen what was coming next? What if they had a guide that would tell them what to expect and how to be ready? What if they could anticipate what is predictable about the high school years before they actually hit? These Phase Guides give a parent that kind of preparation so they can have a plan when they need it most."

JOSH SHIPP
AUTHOR, TEEN EXPERT, AND YOUTH SPEAKER

"The Phase Guides are incredibly creative, well researched, and filled with inspirational actions for everyday life. Each age-specific guide is catalytic for equipping parents to lead and love their kids as they grow up. I'm blown away and deeply encouraged by the content and by its creators. I highly recommend Phase resources for all parents, teachers, and influencers of children. This is the stuff that challenges us and changes our world. Get them. Read them. And use them!"

DANIELLE STRICKLAND
OFFICER WITH THE SALVATION ARMY, AUTHOR, SPEAKER, MOTHER OF TWO

"It's true that parenting is one of life's greatest joys but it is not without its challenges. If we're honest, parenting can sometimes feel like trying to choreograph a dance to an ever-changing beat. It can be clumsy and riddled with well-meaning missteps. If parenting is a dance, this Parenting Guide is a skilled instructor refining your technique and helping you move gracefully to a steady beat. For those of us who love to plan ahead, this guide will help you anticipate what's to come so you can be poised and ready to embrace the moments you want to enjoy."

TINA NAIDOO
MSSW, LCSW EXECUTIVE DIRECTOR, THE POTTER'S HOUSE OF DALLAS, INC.

PARENTING YOUR EIGHTH GRADER

A GUIDE TO MAKING THE MOST OF THE "YEAH . . . I KNOW" PHASE

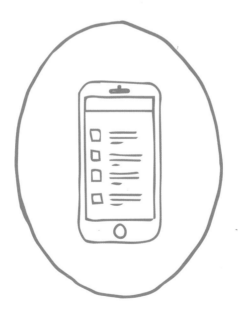

KRISTEN IVY AND REGGIE JOINER

PARENTING YOUR EIGHTH GRADER
A GUIDE TO MAKING THE MOST OF THE "YEAH ... I KNOW" PHASE

Published by Orange, a division of The reThink Group, Inc.,
5870 Charlotte Lane, Suite 300,
Cumming, GA 30040 U.S.A.

©2017 Kristen Ivy and Reggie Joiner
Authors: Kristen Ivy and Reggie Joiner
Lead Editor: Karen Wilson
Editing Team: Melanie Williams, Hannah Crosby, Sherry Surratt

Art Direction: Ryan Boon and Hannah Crosby
Book Design: FiveStone and Sharon van Rossum

Printed in the United States of America
First Edition 2017
1 2 3 4 5 6 7 8 9 10

Special thanks to:

Jim Burns, Ph.D for guidance and consultation on having conversations about sexual integrity

Jon Acuff for guidance and consultation on having conversations about technological responsibility

Jean Sumner, MD for guidance and consultation on having conversations about healthy habits

Every educator, counselor, community leader, and researcher who invested in the Phase Project

TABLE OF CONTENTS

HOW TO USE THIS ~~BOOK~~ ~~JOURNAL~~ GUIDE

The guide you hold in your hand doesn't have very many words, but it does have a lot of ideas. Some of these ideas come from thousands of hours of research. Others come from parents, educators, and volunteers who spend every day with kids the same age as yours. This guide won't tell you everything about your kid, but it will tell you a few things about kids at this age.

The best way to use this guide is to take what these pages tell you about eighth graders and combine it with what you know is true about *your* eighth grader.

Let's sum it up:

THINGS ABOUT EIGHTH GRADERS +
THOUGHTS ABOUT *YOUR* EIGHTH GRADER =
YOUR GUIDE TO THE NEXT 52 WEEKS OF PARENTING

After each idea in this guide, there are pages with a few questions designed to prompt you to think about your kid, your family, and yourself as a parent. The only guarantee we give to parents who use this guide is this: You will mess up some things as a parent this year. Actually, that's a guarantee to every parent, regardless. But you, you picked up this book! You want to be a better parent. And that's what we hope this guide will do: help you parent your eighth grader just a little better, simply because you paused to consider a few ideas that can help you make the most of this phase.

THE EIGHTH GRADE PHASE

Congratulations! You're officially in the "home stretch" of middle school!

After surviving seventh grade, you might be thinking, "Praise the Lord! The end of the tunnel is in sight and middle school is almost over." But don't rush past this year too quickly. Eighth grade may be the very best year yet.

Something incredible happens as your kid rounds the corner from seventh to eighth grade. Uncertainty becomes confidence. "I need you" becomes, "I've got this." And with a much stronger sense of self, your kid begins moving from "what is" to "what could be."

Sure, eye rolls, huffing sounds, and slamming doors might still be some of their chosen communication tools, but don't mistake that for how they also feel. Eighth graders are complex. They feel a lot of things. Yeah, they rolled their eyes at you—they had to show you some expression of what they think. But they also did what you asked. And they actually care pretty deeply what you think about them. That's the tension. They still want your approval, but they also know they have to be who they were created to be. They have to become their own person. And that means a little more independence, a little more self-expression, and a little more personal choice.

Eighth graders don't always want to talk to you, but they do desire real conversation. They may still be highly brand-conscious and spend way too long on their hair in the morning, but they also want authenticity in their relationships. They may delete a social media post if it doesn't get the appropriate number of likes, but they're also craving deeper connection. They're in this incredible "middle space," which includes self-discovery, deeper thinking, and genuine transformation. And it's in this space that we get a glimpse of who they could be.

As your eighth grader becomes a little more comfortable in their own skin, you'll have a front row seat to watch them hit new levels of independence and turn the corner toward adulthood. But, they still need you. They're not ready to be totally independent just yet. So, watch as they go . . . and wait in the wings for the moments when they look to you for direction or support.

Watch as they run squealing to hug their friends they just saw yesterday. And be the hug that's waiting for them when they feel left out.

Watch their sense of humor grow and witness their discovery of sarcasm. And be the first to talk it through with them when someone else's cutting humor stings.

Watch as they take risks, try something new, or step out in faith. And be there to motivate them to try again if they crash and burn.

Watch them expand their thinking and make their faith personal. And be the safe place they can process their fears or doubts.

Watch them discover that they're wired for a purpose. And be the one to remind them what you see in them when they forget.

Watch as they're becoming a young adult—almost overnight. And wait for the moment when they need to crawl back into your arms for comfort.

Eighth grade has so many possibilities. So much opportunity. Yes, the end of middle school may be in sight, but avoid the temptation to fast forward this phase. It just might end up being your favorite.

- KATIE EDWARDS
AUTHOR, COMMUNICATOR, & JUNIOR HIGH PASTOR AT SADDLEBACK CHURCH (ALSO, A MOM WHO HAS BEEN THROUGH THIS MIDDLE SCHOOL PHASE)

52
WEEKS

—

TO PARENT YOUR
EIGHTH GRADER

WHEN YOU SEE
HOW MUCH

Time

YOU HAVE LEFT

—

YOU TEND TO DO

More

WITH THE TIME
YOU HAVE NOW.

THERE ARE APPROXIMATELY

936 WEEKS

FROM THE TIME A BABY IS BORN
UNTIL THEY GROW UP AND MOVE TO
WHATEVER IS NEXT.

On the day your kid starts eighth grade, you only have 260 weeks remaining. You may feel as if you can watch time moving—simply by how quickly your middle schooler is growing and changing and becoming someone new before your eyes. You don't need another reminder that your kid is growing up—*fast*.

Every week counts. Of course, each week might not feel significant. There may be weeks this year when all you feel like you accomplished was stalking their social media accounts after they go to bed.

Take a deep breath.
You don't have to get everything done this week.

But what happens in your child's life week after week, year after year, adds up. So, it might be a good idea to put a number to your weeks.

MEASURE IT OUT.

Write down the number of weeks that have already passed since your eighth grader was born. Then write down the number of weeks you have left before they potentially graduate high school.

HINT: If you want a little help counting it out, you can download the free Parent Cue app on all mobile platforms.

_____

_____

_____

CREATE A VISUAL COUNTDOWN.

 Find a jar and fill it with one marble for each week you have remaining with your eighth grader. Then remove one marble every week as a reminder to make the most of your time.

Where can you place your visual countdown so you will see it frequently?

_____

_____

_____

_____

_____

Which day of the week is best for you to remove a marble?

_____

_____

_____

Is there anything you want to do each week as you remove a marble? *(Examples: say a prayer, write your kid a note, retell one favorite memory from this past week)*

_____

_____

_____

_____

_____

_____

_____

_____

_____

_____

_____

_____

EVERY PHASE IS A
TIMEFRAME
IN A KID'S LIFE
WHEN YOU CAN
LEVERAGE
DISTINCTIVE
OPPORTUNITIES
TO INFLUENCE
THEIR

future.

YOU ONLY HAVE
52 WEEKS
WITH YOUR EIGHTH GRADER

while they are still in eighth grade.

Then they will be in ninth grade,

and you will never know them as an eighth grader again.

Or, to say it another way:

Before you know it, your teenager will . . .

voice their political opinion.

challenge your religious views.

take up a social cause (probably to loosen curfew regulations).

The point is this: The phase you are in now has remarkable potential. And before the end of eighth grade, there are some distinctive opportunities you don't want to miss. So, as you count down the next 52 weeks, pay attention to what makes these weeks uniquely different from the time you've already spent together and the weeks you will have when they move on to the next phase.

What are some things you have noticed about your eighth grader in this phase that you really enjoy?

_____

_____

_____

_____

_____

_____

_____

_____

_____

_____

_____

_____

_____

_____

_____

_____

_____

_____

_____

_____

What is something new you are learning as a parent during this phase?

_____

_____

_____

_____

_____

_____

_____

_____

_____

_____

_____

_____

_____

_____

_____

_____

_____

_____

_____

_____

_____

EIGHTH GRADE

—

THE PHASE WHEN IT'S COOL TO HAVE CHOICES, IT'S NOT COOL TO ANSWER QUESTIONS, AND ONE SMART KID WILL REMIND YOU, *"Yeah . . . I know."*

GIVE OPTIONS WHENEVER POSSIBLE.

Remember when you had a two-year-old who wanted to "do it myself?" Your teenager's resistance may not come in the form of a toddler tantrum, but the emotions may feel familiar. Whenever possible, give options so they have some freedom to choose.

RE-DEFINE THE CONVERSATION.

Your eighth grader may answer your questions with one word, an eye-roll, or an all-too-clear facial expression. But don't mistranslate the cues. Eighth graders actually want to have adult conversations sometimes. Be available—even if it seems a little pointless.

EIGHTH GRADERS ARE SMART.

In fact, there may be no phase quite as smart as this one—just ask them. Being so much smarter than everyone else can really become a burden. Sometimes their patience just runs out, and they simply can't explain it to you one more time. On some occasions, have fun going toe-to-toe with your eighth grader and challenge them back. Just remember, the important thing is how they personalize what they believe in this phase. So encourage their personal discoveries.

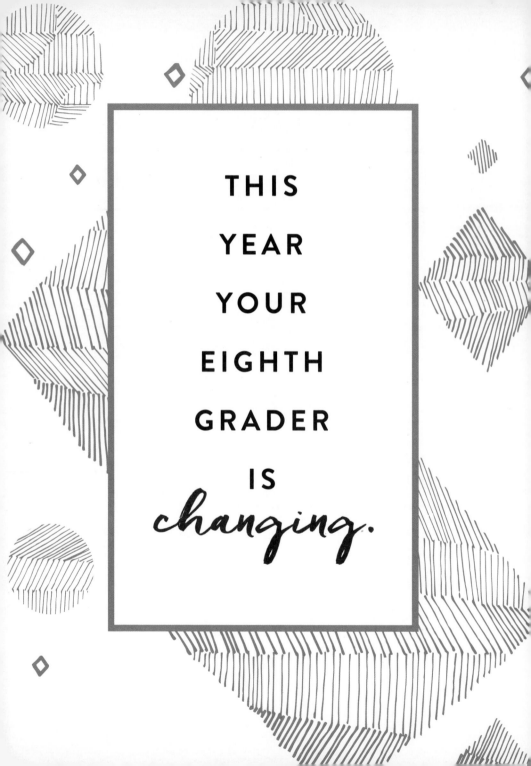

THIS
YEAR
YOUR
EIGHTH
GRADER
IS
changing.

PHYSICALLY

- Needs 9-11 hours of sleep each night and may easily fatigue or develop headaches
- Girls outpace guys in development
- Guys experience changes in height and body shape, and may develop body odor, body hair, and increased muscle mass
- Girls experience a significant growth spurt, development of body odor, body hair, and breasts, and menstruation is likely (10-16 years)

MENTALLY

- Capable of self-evaluation and self-critique
- Able to see two sides of an argument
- Enjoys forming and sharing their opinion
- Growing ability to organize

SOCIALLY

- Often interested in pop culture, slang, current events, or politics
- Wants to negotiate rules
- Displays an increasingly adult-like personality
- Needs non-parental adult influences
- More concerned about personal appearance than personal environment (like the state of their locker or bedroom)

EMOTIONALLY

- Enjoys sarcasm and sophisticated jokes
- Often interested in leadership roles and teaching younger children
- May emphasize physical appearance and performance
- Tends to overschedule their time
- Often feels more comfortable in their own skin

What are some changes you are noticing in your eighth grader?

_____

_____

_____

_____

_____

_____

_____

You may disagree with some of the characteristics we've shared about eighth graders. That's because every eighth grader is unique. What makes your eighth grader different from eighth graders in general?

_____

_____

_____

_____

_____

_____

_____

_____

What are some things that impress you about your eighth grader?

Mark this page. Some weeks it may be easy to focus only on what your eighth grader does wrong, so try to catch them doing something right. Write it down here. If you want to be really thorough, there are about 52 blank lines.

_____

_____

_____

_____

_____

_____

_____

_____

_____

_____

_____

_____

_____

_____

_____

_____

_____

_____

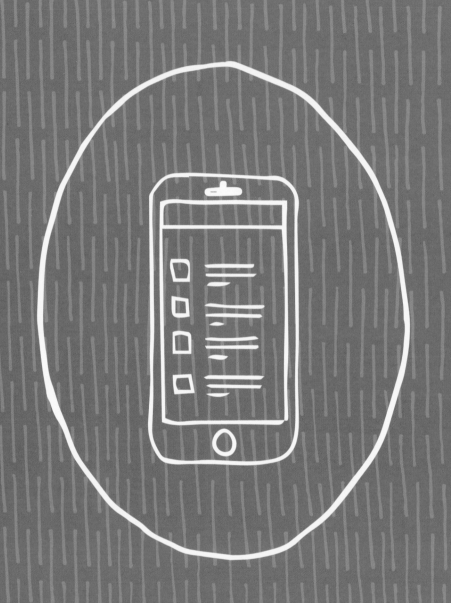

SIX
THINGS
—
EVERY KID
NEEDS

YOUR KID
NEEDS **6** THINGS
OVER TIME

LOVE
STORIES
WORDS WORK
PEOPLE
FUN

OVER THE NEXT 260 WEEKS, YOUR EIGHTH GRADER WILL NEED MANY THINGS:

Some of the things your kid needs will change from phase to phase, but there are six things every kid needs at every phase. In fact, these things may be the most important things you give your kid.

EVERY KID, AT EVERY PHASE, NEEDS . . .

♡ LOVE
to give them a
sense of WORTH.

▥ STORIES
to give them a bigger
PERSPECTIVE.

⫘ WORK
to give them
PURPOSE.

♟ FUN
to give them
CONNECTION.

👥 PEOPLE
to give them
BELONGING.

▤ WORDS
to give them
DIRECTION.

The next few pages are designed to help you think about how you will give your child these six things, right now—while they are in eighth grade.

EVERY KID

NEEDS

love

OVER TIME

—

TO GIVE THEM

A SENSE OF

worth.

 ONE QUESTION YOUR EIGHTH GRADER IS ASKING

Your eighth grader is cool. No longer at the mercy of an uncontrollable emotional outburst, eighth graders are increasingly able to self-regulate their actions, emotions, and activities. But, this emerging sense of control creates a new kind of tension for your teenager to resolve.

Your eighth grader is asking one major question:

"WHO DO I WANT TO BE?"

Eighth graders enjoy setting a personal goal and working to achieve it. Their ambitions may outweigh their practical application to a task, but most teenagers in this phase are eager to do something significant. That's why one of the best ways to build your eighth grader's sense of worth is to do one thing:

AFFIRM their personal journey.

When you affirm their personal journey, you communicate . . .

"You can make a difference at your school,"

"You can make a difference in our community,"

and "You can make a difference in our family."

In order to affirm your eighth grader, you need time together.
What are some times during your week when you connect best?
(Examples: the commute to school, eating a meal together,
driving their friends, family game or movie night.)

_____

_____

_____

_____

_____

_____

_____

_____

_____

_____

_____

_____

_____

_____

_____

_____

_____

_____

Affirming your eighth grader requires paying attention to what they like. What does your eighth grader seem to enjoy the most right now? *(If you don't know, it's okay to ask them.)*

_____

_____

_____

_____

_____

_____

_____

_____

_____

_____

_____

_____

_____

_____

_____

_____

_____

_____

How might you try to rediscover what they like—even though it's changing often?

_____

_____

_____

_____

_____

_____

_____

_____

_____

_____

_____

_____

_____

_____

_____

_____

_____

_____

_____

It's impossible to consistently love someone as challenging as your eighth grader unless you have a little time for yourself. What can you do to refuel each week so you are able to give your eighth grader the love they need?

_____

_____

_____

_____

_____

_____

_____

_____

_____

_____

_____

_____

_____

_____

_____

_____

_____

EVERY KID

NEEDS

stories

OVER TIME

—

TO GIVE THEM

A BIGGER

perspective.

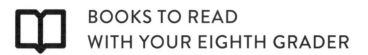 BOOKS TO READ
WITH YOUR EIGHTH GRADER

THE BOY IN THE STRIPED PAJAMAS
by John Boyne

FAHRENHEIT 451
by Ray Bradbury

ENDER'S GAME
by Orson Scott Card

MY ANTONIA
by Willa Cather

ARTEMIS FOWL
by Eoin Colfer

THE HUNGER GAMES (SERIES)
by Suzanne Collins

THE MAZE RUNNER (SERIES)
by James Dashner

OUT OF AFRICA
by Isak Dinesen

THE HOUSE OF THE SCORPION
by Nancy Farmer

FLOWERS FOR ALGERNON
by Daniel Keyes

THE CALL OF THE WILD
by Jack London

THE GIVER
by Lois Lowry

CINDER (SERIES)
by Marissa Meyer

DIVERGENT (SERIES)
by Veronica Roth

ROLL OF THUNDER, HEAR MY CRY
by Mildred D. Taylor

THE HIDING PLACE
by Corrie Ten Boom

THE UNLIKELY HERO OF ROOM 13B
by Teresa Toten

HOMECOMING
by Cynthia Voigt

UGLIES
by Scott Westerfeld

BROWN GIRL DREAMING
by Jacqueline Woodson

Share a story. Whether it's a book, play, TV series, or movie, what are some stories that engage your eighth grader?

_____

_____

_____

_____

_____

_____

_____

_____

_____

_____

_____

_____

_____

_____

_____

_____

_____

_____

_____

What might happen to your relationship when you watch or read the same story together?

_____

_____

_____

_____

_____

_____

_____

_____

_____

_____

_____

_____

_____

_____

_____

_____

_____

_____

_____

Tell a story. What are some personal or family stories you could share with your eighth grader to help shape their perspective about friendship, growing up, and personal values this year?

_____

_____

_____

_____

_____

_____

_____

_____

_____

_____

_____

_____

_____

_____

_____

_____

_____

_____

_____

Live a story. When an eighth grader serves others, they learn about someone else's story. This is an important phase for your kid to experience serving others. Is there a global service opportunity you could participate in with them this year?

EVERY KID

NEEDS

work

OVER TIME

——

TO GIVE

THEM

purpose.

WORK YOUR
EIGHTH GRADER CAN DO

**DO HOMEWORK
INDEPENDENTLY**

**SWEEP AND MOP
THE FLOOR**

MOW LAWNS
(yours or someone else's)

USE A CORDLESS DRILL

**LOOK AFTER SIBLINGS
OR MAYBE BABYSIT**

**HELP SHOP
FOR GROCERIES**

USE KITCHEN KNIVES

**TAKE OUT THE TRASH /
RECYCLING**

**FROST A CAKE /
CUPCAKES**

**START, MANAGE, AND
PUT OUT A FIRE**
(the kind that happens in
controlled spaces, and only
after instruction and practice)

**HELP WITH PLUMBING,
DRYWALL, OR PAINTING
THE HOME**

**PRACTICE A SPORT,
MUSICAL INSTRUMENT,
OR OTHER SKILL**

What are some ways your eighth grader already shows responsibility at home, at school, and in-between?

_____

_____

_____

_____

_____

_____

_____

_____

_____

_____

_____

_____

_____

_____

_____

_____

_____

_____

_____

How can you collaborate with your eighth grader to agree on which of their responsibilities matter most for your family and their future?

_____

_____

_____

_____

_____

_____

_____

_____

_____

_____

_____

_____

_____

_____

_____

_____

_____

_____

Some days might be easier than others to motivate your eighth grader. What are some strategies you could employ to keep your eighth grader motivated?

_____

_____

_____

_____

_____

_____

_____

_____

_____

_____

_____

_____

_____

_____

_____

_____

_____

_____

What are things you hope your eighth grader will be able to do independently when they get to high school? How are you helping them develop those skills now?

_____

_____

_____

_____

_____

_____

_____

_____

_____

_____

_____

_____

_____

_____

_____

_____

_____

_____

EVERY KID

NEEDS

fun

OVER TIME

—

TO GIVE

THEM

connection.

WAYS TO HAVE FUN WITH YOUR EIGHTH GRADER

BOARD GAMES:

CATCH PHRASE®

APPLES TO APPLES®

BALDERDASH®

SAY ANYTHING®

TABOO®

SCATTERGORIES®

BEEN THERE, DONE THAT®

RUMMIKUB®

CARD GAMES:

SPOONS

SLAP JACK

CRAZY EIGHTS

B.S. / I DOUBT IT

GAME OF THINGS

PHASE 10

ACTIVITIES:

ART CLASS

COOKING CLASS

WOODWORKING CLASS

LOCAL MUSEUMS / THEATER

WATER PARK

LOCAL SPORTING EVENT

HIKING

TRAIN FOR A 5K

"WOULD YOU RATHER?"

DRIVE-IN MOVIE

LONG BOARDING

APP GAMES (compete against each other)

KAYAKING

AN ESCAPE ROOM

PROGRESSIVE DINNER

FISHING

OUTDOOR CONCERTS

VISITS TO A HISTORICAL MARKER

COACH A LITTLE LEAGUE TEAM TOGETHER

What are some activities your eighth grader enjoys that you could do as a family (and maybe sometimes include their friends)?

_____

_____

_____

_____

_____

_____

_____

_____

_____

_____

_____

_____

_____

_____

_____

_____

_____

_____

_____

_____

_____

What are some activities your eighth grader enjoys that you could occasionally do together, one-on-one?

_____

_____

_____

_____

_____

_____

_____

When are the best times of the day, or week, for you to set aside to just have fun with your eighth grader?

_____

_____

_____

_____

_____

_____

_____

_____

Some days are *extra* fun days. What are some ways you want to celebrate the special days coming up this year?

NEXT BIRTHDAY

_____

_____

_____

_____

_____

_____

_____

_____

_____

_____

_____

_____

_____

_____

_____

_____

_____

HOLIDAYS

Consider celebrating a few random holidays: the first/last day of school, National Donut Day, Hamburger Month.

EVERY KID

NEEDS

people

OVER TIME

—

TO GIVE

THEM

belonging.

ADULTS WHO MIGHT INFLUENCE YOUR EIGHTH GRADER

PARENTS

YOUTUBE & CULTURAL ICONS

SCHOOL WORKERS

GRANDPARENTS

FRIENDS' PARENTS

CHURCH LEADERS

AUNTS & UNCLES

EIGHTH GRADE TEACHERS

COACHES & CLUB LEADERS

You already know friends matter to your eighth grader, but it's easy to forget that eighth graders also need other adults in their community. List at least five adults who have the potential to positively influence your eighth grader.

_____

_____

_____

_____

_____

_____

_____

_____

_____

_____

_____

_____

_____

_____

_____

_____

What is one thing these adults could do for your eighth grader this year?

_____

_____

_____

_____

_____

_____

_____

_____

_____

_____

_____

_____

_____

_____

_____

_____

_____

_____

_____

What are a few ways you could show these adults appreciation for the significant role they play in your kid's life?

_____

_____

_____

_____

_____

_____

_____

_____

_____

_____

_____

_____

_____

_____

_____

_____

_____

_____

_____

 # WORDS YOUR EIGHTH GRADER NEEDS TO HEAR

GOOD MORNING!

I'M SORRY

WHAT DO YOU THINK?

I HOPE YOU KNOW . . .

TELL ME MORE

DON'T BE MEAN

I HAVE NOTICED . . .

YOU CAN DO THIS

I LOVE YOU

I WAS THINKING ABOUT YOU

I'M REALLY PROUD WHEN . . .

GOOD NIGHT!

WANT A HUG?

YOU WILL DO WELL NEXT YEAR BECAUSE . . .

BE YOURSELF

YOU ARE BEAUTIFUL / HANDSOME

YOU'RE ENOUGH

THANKS FOR TRUSTING ME

ME TOO

What are some ways you can share personal and specific encouragement with your seventh grader?

Hint: You might start with the things that impress you about your kid from page 27.

_____

_____

_____

_____

_____

_____

_____

_____

_____

_____

_____

_____

_____

_____

_____

_____

_____

_____

Many middle schoolers are inspired by words from a song lyric, quote, or Scripture. How can you discover the words that mean something to your middle schooler?

_____

_____

_____

_____

_____

_____

_____

_____

_____

_____

_____

_____

_____

_____

_____

_____

_____

What are some quotes, lyrics, Scriptures, or inspirational thoughts you want to share with your sixth grader? How might you share those in a way that resonates with them?

_____

_____

_____

_____

_____

_____

_____

_____

_____

_____

_____

_____

_____

_____

_____

_____

_____

_____

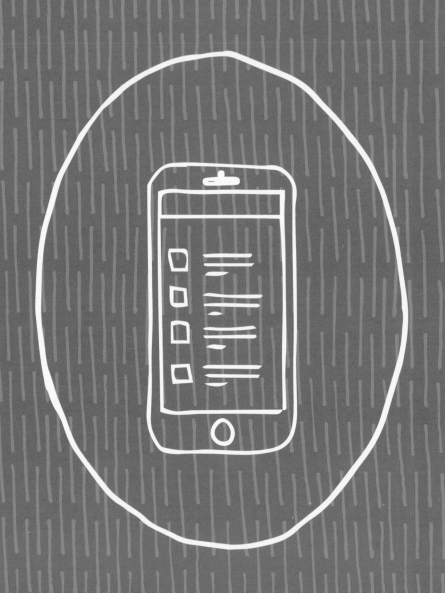

FOUR CONVERSATIONS

—

TO HAVE IN THIS PHASE

WHEN YOU KNOW
WHERE YOU WANT
TO GO,

AND YOU KNOW
WHERE YOU ARE
NOW,

YOU CAN ALWAYS
DO SOMETHING

TO MOVE IN A
BETTER DIRECTION.

OVER THE NEXT 260 WEEKS OF YOUR CHILD'S LIFE, SOME CONVERSATIONS MAY MATTER MORE THAN OTHERS.

WHAT YOU SAY, FOR EXAMPLE, REGARDING . . .

Music Genres

Clothing Brands

and Sports Teams

MIGHT HAVE LESS IMPACT ON THEIR FUTURE THAN WHAT YOU SAY REGARDING . . .

Health

Sex

Technology

or Faith.

The next pages are about the conversations that matter most. On the left page is a destination—what you might want to be true in your kid's life 260 weeks from now. On the right page is a goal for conversations with your eighth grader this year and a few suggestions about what you might want to say.

Healthy habits

—

LEARNING TO STRENGTHEN MY BODY THROUGH EXERCISE, NUTRITION, AND SELF-ADVOCACY

THIS YEAR YOU WILL

DEVELOP POSITIVE ROUTINES

SO YOUR EIGHTH GRADER WILL VALUE THEIR CHANGING BODY AND MAINTAIN GOOD HYGIENE.

Some healthy habits happen without conversation—just by exercising and playing outside with your eighth grader, and scheduling a physical once per year. You can also improve your eighth grader's habits with a few simple words.

SAY THINGS LIKE . . .

WHAT DO YOUR FRIENDS SAY ABOUT ALCOHOL?
(Talk about drugs and alcohol.)

"WHAT WOULD YOU LIKE FOR DINNER THIS WEEK?"
(Let them participate in dinner plans, and eat together whenever possible.)

"HOW DO I KNOW IF THIS IS HEALTHY?"
(Use websites like MayoClinic.org to look up information about health together.)

"LET'S DO THIS TOGETHER."
(Exercise or begin a healthy eating plan together.)

"IT'S TIME TO TURN IT OFF AND GO TO BED."
(Teens need 9-11 hours of sleep.)

"HOW CAN I HELP YOU FEEL LESS STRESSED?"
(Help them regulate their emotional health.)

"WHEN WAS THE LAST TIME YOU DRANK SOME WATER?"
(Middle schoolers sometimes forget to stay hydrated when exercising—*or when breathing.*)

What are some activities you can do with your eighth grader that require a little bit of exercise?

_____

_____

_____

_____

_____

_____

_____

_____

_____

_____

_____

_____

_____

_____

_____

_____

_____

_____

_____

Eighth graders can be sensitive about their body. What's one way you can promote a healthy body image for your eighth grader?

_____

_____

_____

_____

_____

_____

_____

_____

_____

_____

_____

_____

_____

_____

_____

_____

_____

_____

Kids who cook learn what ingredients are in the things they eat. What are some simple ways your eighth grader can help you in the kitchen?

_____

_____

_____

_____

_____

_____

_____

_____

_____

_____

_____

_____

_____

_____

_____

_____

_____

_____

What are your own health goals for this year? How can you improve the habits in your own life?

_____

_____

_____

_____

_____

_____

_____

_____

_____

_____

_____

_____

_____

_____

_____

_____

_____

_____

Sexual integrity

—

GUARDING MY

POTENTIAL FOR

INTIMACY THROUGH

APPROPRIATE

BOUNDARIES

AND MUTUAL

RESPECT

FOUR CONVERSATIONS TO HAVE IN THIS PHASE

THIS YEAR YOU WILL

INTERPRET WHAT IS CHANGING

SO YOUR EIGHTH GRADER WILL RESPECT THEMSELVES AND GROW IN CONFIDENCE.

Your eighth grader may find themselves in a situation that creates tension between what they have always believed and what they feel in the moment. Talk with your teen about what is changing socially as it relates to pressures, opportunities, and expectations.

SAY THINGS LIKE . . .

WHEN JON COMMENTED ON YOUR POST, WHAT DID HE MEAN BY . . . ?
(Stay curious about what's happening in their world.)

"I'M HERE IF YOU WANT TO TALK."

"IF YOU EVER FEEL LIKE SOMEONE IS WANTING YOU TO DO SOMETHING YOU DON'T WANT TO DO, YOU COULD ALWAYS SAY . . ."
(Help them script responses to difficult situations.)

"THANK YOU FOR TALKING ABOUT THIS. CAN WE TALK ABOUT IT AGAIN ANOTHER TIME?"
(Always finish the conversation with room to pick it back up again later.)

"I'M SO GLAD YOU TOLD ME."

"YOU ARE BRAVE TO SHARE THAT."
(Take what they say and feel seriously.)

"WHO DO YOU KNOW THAT IS DATING?"

WHAT DOES DATING MEAN?"

When it comes to your kid's sexuality, what do you hope is true for them 260 weeks from now?

_____

_____

_____

_____

_____

_____

_____

_____

_____

_____

_____

_____

_____

_____

_____

_____

_____

_____

_____

What are the biggest points of tension with your eighth grader when it comes to modesty, sexual language, dating, peer pressure, or issues of sexual integrity? Who can you go to for advice on these issues?

_____

_____

_____

_____

_____

_____

_____

_____

_____

_____

_____

_____

_____

_____

_____

_____

_____

Be prepared. By the beginning of ninth grade, 30% of teens report being sexually active. Pause. Breathe. Now, write down two or three things you want to say to your kid if you were to discover something you hadn't expected when it comes to their sexuality.

_____

_____

_____

_____

_____

_____

_____

_____

_____

_____

_____

_____

_____

_____

_____

_____

_____

When your eighth grader has questions they won't ask you, who do you hope they will go to for advice?

HINT: Whoever that person is, let them know. And let your eighth grader know.

_____

_____

_____

_____

_____

_____

_____

_____

_____

_____

_____

_____

_____

_____

_____

_____

_____

_____

_____

_____

Technological responsibility

—

LEVERAGING THE
POTENTIAL OF ONLINE
EXPERIENCES TO
ENHANCE MY OFFLINE
COMMUNITY
AND SUCCESS

THIS YEAR YOU WILL

COLLABORATE A PLAN

SO YOUR EIGHTH GRADER WILL RESPECT LIMITS AND STRENGTHEN SOCIAL ABILITIES

Your eighth grader publishes content to the world, and the world answers back. Whether they have their own social media accounts or know a friend who does, there's a good chance your eighth grader is connected to about 800 million people you will never meet. That's enough reason to have some conversations.

SAY THINGS LIKE . . .

> **LET'S SET UP THAT ACCOUNT TOGETHER.**

"WHAT DO YOU THINK IS A HEALTHY AMOUNT OF TIME FOR YOU TO SPEND ONLINE?"
(Collaborate on expectations, rules, and consequences.)

"WHAT SHOULD THE PASSWORD BE?"
(When you are ready, set up social media accounts together, and know their passwords.)

"IS IT OKAY IF I COMMENT ON YOUR POSTS?"
(Be considerate about how you engage with them online.)

"WHAT YOU POST IS PUBLIC, EVEN IF IT FEELS PRIVATE, AND IT CAN BE PERMANENT."
(Help them recognize potential risks related to the words, images, and videos they create.)

"I SAW THIS VIDEO AND IT MADE ME THINK OF YOU."
(Use technology to connect throughout the day—with no agenda.)

When it comes to your kid's engagement with technology, what do you hope is true for them 260 weeks from now?

_____

_____

_____

_____

_____

_____

_____

_____

_____

_____

_____

_____

_____

_____

_____

_____

_____

_____

_____

What rules do you have for digital devices in your family? If you don't have any, what are two or three you might want to set for your eighth grader?

_____

_____

_____

_____

_____

_____

_____

_____

_____

_____

_____

_____

_____

_____

_____

_____

_____

_____

_____

What restrictions do you have on your eighth grader's use of mobile devices now that you might not have in phases to come? How might your eighth grader earn more freedom over time?

_____

_____

_____

_____

_____

_____

_____

_____

_____

_____

_____

_____

_____

_____

_____

_____

_____

_____

What are your own personal values and disciplines when it comes to leveraging technology? Are there ways you want to improve your own savvy, skill, or responsibility in this area?

_____

_____

_____

_____

_____

_____

_____

_____

_____

_____

_____

_____

_____

_____

_____

_____

_____

_____

Authentic faith

—

TRUSTING JESUS
IN A WAY THAT
TRANSFORMS HOW
I LOVE GOD,
MYSELF,
AND THE REST
OF THE WORLD

THIS YEAR YOU WILL

PROVOKE DISCOVERY

SO YOUR EIGHTH GRADER WILL OWN THEIR OWN
FAITH AND VALUE A FAITH COMMUNITY.

Your eighth grader wants to discover how faith applies to them, right now. Connect Biblical truth to their everyday world by purchasing a youth Bible, so they have access to articles and devotional copy that can inspire them. And, connect faith to everyday experiences through conversations at home.

SAY THINGS LIKE . . .

WHAT WOULD BE A FUN WAY WE COULD SERVE OTHERS TOGETHER? (Consider serving at your church or a local ministry that appeals to your eighth grader's interests.)

"IN THIS WORLD YOU WILL HAVE TROUBLE. BUT TAKE HEART! I HAVE OVERCOME THE WORLD." John 16:33 (Repeat simple Bible verses.)

"THE WAY YOU LIVE CAN SHOW OTHERS WHO JESUS IS."

"CAN WE PRAY ABOUT THIS TOGETHER?"

"WHEN DO YOU FEEL CLOSEST TO GOD?"

"HOW CAN I PRAY FOR YOU TODAY / THIS WEEK?"

"WHAT'S SOMETHING NEW THAT YOU'RE LEARNING ABOUT GOD?"

"GOD MADE YOU, HE KNOWS YOU, AND HE LOVES YOU."

"THAT'S A GREAT QUESTION. I DON'T KNOW THE ANSWER, BUT WE CAN FIND OUT."

"GOD WILL NEVER STOP LOVING YOU."

What are some ways you can help deepen your eighth grader's connection with friends who follow Jesus?

_____

_____

_____

_____

_____

_____

_____

_____

_____

_____

_____

_____

_____

_____

_____

_____

_____

_____

What are some ways you can help deepen your eighth grader's connection with adults whose faith they admire?

_____

_____

_____

_____

_____

_____

_____

_____

_____

_____

_____

_____

_____

_____

_____

_____

_____

_____

_____

_____

What are some overnight or weekend opportunities provided by your church or a local youth ministry? (*Over the next 260 weeks, prioritize these experiences. Put the dates on the calendar early. Allow them to invite a friend if they are nervous to go "alone." Look for scholarships or help your kid raise money.*)

_____

_____

_____

_____

_____

_____

_____

_____

_____

_____

_____

_____

_____

_____

_____

What routines or habits do you have in your own life that are stretching your faith?

_____

_____

_____

_____

_____

_____

_____

_____

_____

_____

_____

_____

_____

_____

_____

_____

_____

_____

_____

THE

rhythm

OF YOUR

WEEK

—

WILL SHAPE

THE VALUES

IN YOUR

home.

NOW THAT YOU HAVE FILLED THIS BOOK WITH IDEAS AND GOALS, IT MAY SEEM AS IF YOU WILL NEVER HAVE TIME TO GET IT ALL DONE.

Actually, you have *260 weeks*.

And every week has potential.

The secret to making the most of this phase is to take advantage of the time you already have. On average, you probably spend around four hours each day with your middle schooler. (In high school that number will drop in half.) So, make the most of these four times together.

Instill purpose by starting the day with encouraging words.

Interpret life during informal conversations as you travel.

Establish values with intentional conversations while you eat together.

Listen to their heart by staying available—just in case.

How are you adjusting to a new rhythm in this phase?

_____

_____

_____

_____

_____

_____

_____

_____

_____

_____

_____

_____

_____

_____

_____

_____

_____

_____

_____

_____

What are some of your favorite routines with your eighth grader?

_____

_____

_____

_____

_____

_____

_____

_____

_____

_____

_____

_____

_____

_____

_____

_____

_____

_____

_____

_____

_____

Write down any other thoughts or questions about parenting your eighth grader.

_____

_____

_____

_____

_____

_____

_____

_____

_____

_____

_____

_____

_____

_____

_____

_____

_____

_____

_____

YOU HAVE

APPROXIMATELY

260 WEEKS.

IT'S JUST
A PHASE
SO DON'T
MISS IT.

ABOUT THE AUTHORS

KRISTEN IVY @kristen_ivy

Kristen Ivy is executive director of the Phase Project. She and her husband, Matt, are in the preschool and elementary phases with three kids: Sawyer, Hensley, and Raleigh.

Kristen earned her Bachelors of Education from Baylor University in 2004 and received a Master of Divinity from Mercer University in 2009. She worked in the public school system as a high school biology and English teacher, where she learned firsthand the importance of influencing the next generation.

Kristen is also the President at Orange and has played an integral role in the development of the elementary, middle school, and high school curriculum and has shared her experiences at speaking events across the country. She is the co-author of *Playing for Keeps*, *Creating a Lead Small Culture*, *It's Just a Phase*, and *Don't Miss It*.

REGGIE JOINER @reggiejoiner

Reggie Joiner is founder and CEO of the reThink Group and co-founder of the Phase Project. He and his wife, Debbie, have reared four kids into adulthood. They now also have two grandchildren.

The reThink Group (also known as Orange) is a non-profit organization whose purpose is to influence those who influence the next generation. Orange provides resources and training for churches and organizations that create environments for parents, kids, and teenagers.

Before starting the reThink Group in 2006, Reggie was one of the founders of North Point Community Church. During his 11 years with Andy Stanley, Reggie was the executive director of family ministry, where he developed a new concept for relevant ministry to children, teenagers, and married adults. Reggie has authored and co-authored more than 10 books including: *Think Orange*, *Seven Practices of Effective Ministry*, *Parenting Beyond Your Capacity*, *Playing for Keeps*, *Lead Small*, *Creating a Lead Small Culture*, and his latest, *A New Kind of Leader* and *Don't Miss It*.

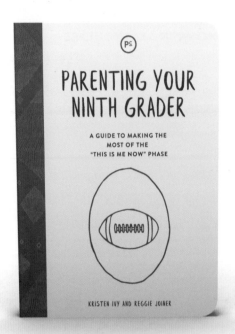

MAKE THE MOST OF EVERY PHASE IN YOUR CHILD'S LIFE

The guide in your hand is one of an eighteen-part series.

So, unless you've figured out a way to freeze time and keep your eighth grader from turning into a ninth grader, you might want to check out the next guide in this set.

Designed in partnership with Parent Cue, each guide will help you rediscover . . .

**what's changing about your kid,
the 6 things your kid needs most,
and 4 conversations to have each year.**

ORDER NOW AT: **WWW.PHASEGUIDES.COM**

WANT TO GIFT A FRIEND WITH ALL 18 GUIDES
OR HAVE ALL THE GUIDES ON HAND FOR YOURSELF?

ORDER THE ENTIRE SERIES
OF PHASE GUIDES TODAY.

"It's hard to connect with your child without first understanding where they are. As counselors and speakers at parenting events across the country, we spend a great deal of time teaching parents about development. To know *where* your child is—not just physically, but emotionally, socially, and spiritually, helps you to truly know and understand *who* your child is. And that understanding is the key to connecting. The Phase Guides give you the tools to do just that. Our wise friends Reggie and Kristen have put together an insightful, hopeful, practical, and literal year-by-year guide that will help you to understand and connect with your child at every age."

SISSY GOFF
M.ED., LPC-MHSP, DIRECTOR OF CHILD & ADOLESCENT COUNSELING AT DAYSTAR COUNSELING MINISTRIES IN NASHVILLE, TENNESSEE, SPEAKER AND AUTHOR OF ARE MY KIDS ON TRACK?

"These resources for parents are fantastically empowering, absolute in their simplicity, and completely doable in every way. The hard work that has gone into the Phase Project will echo through the next generation of children in powerful ways."

JENNIFER WALKER
RN BSN, AUTHOR AND FOUNDER OF MOMS ON CALL

"We all know where we want to end up in our parenting, but how to get there can seem like an unsolved mystery. Through the Phase Project series, Reggie Joiner and Kristen Ivy team up to help us out. The result is a resource that guides us through the different seasons of raising children, and provides a road map to parenting in such a way that we finish up with very few regrets."

SANDRA STANLEY
FOSTER CARE ADVOCATE, BLOGGER, WIFE TO ANDY STANLEY, MOTHER OF THREE

"Not only are the Phase Guides the most creative and well-thought-out guides to parenting I have ever encountered, these books are ESSENTIAL to my daily parenting. With a 13-year-old, 11-year-old, and 9-year-old at home, I am swimming in their wake of daily drama and delicacy. These books are a reminder to enjoy every second. Because it's just a phase."

CARLOS WHITTAKER
AUTHOR, SPEAKER, FATHER OF THREE

"As the founder of Minnie's Food Pantry, I see thousands of people each month with children who will benefit from the advice, guidance, and nuggets of information on how to celebrate and understand the phases of their child's life. Too often we feel like we're losing our mind when sweet little Johnny starts to change his behavior into a person we do not know. I can't wait to start implementing the principles of these books with my clients to remind them . . . it's just a phase."

CHERYL JACKSON
FOUNDER OF MINNIE'S FOOD PANTRY, AWARD-WINNING PHILANTHROPIST, AND GRANDMOTHER

"I began exploring this resource with my counselor hat on, thinking how valuable this will be for the many parents I spend time with in my office. I ended up taking my counselor hat off and putting on my parent hat. Then I kept thinking about friends who are teachers, coaches, youth pastors, and children's ministers, who would want this in their hands. What a valuable resource the Orange team has given us to better understand and care for the kids and adolescents we love. I look forward to sharing it broadly."

DAVID THOMAS
LMSW, DIRECTOR OF FAMILY COUNSELING, DAYSTAR COUNSELING MINISTRIES, SPEAKER AND AUTHOR OF ARE MY KIDS ON TRACK? AND WILD THINGS: THE ART OF NURTURING BOYS

"I have always wished someone would hand me a manual for parenting. Well, the Phase Guides are more than what I wished for. They guide, inspire, and challenge me as a parent—while giving me incredible insight into my children at each age and phase. Our family will be using these every year!"

COURTNEY DEFEO
AUTHOR OF IN THIS HOUSE, WE WILL GIGGLE, MOTHER OF TWO

"As I speak to high school students and their parents, I always wonder to myself: What would it have been like if they had better seen what was coming next? What if they had a guide that would tell them what to expect and how to be ready? What if they could anticipate what is predictable about the high school years before they actually hit? These Phase Guides give a parent that kind of preparation so they can have a plan when they need it most."

JOSH SHIPP
AUTHOR, TEEN EXPERT, AND YOUTH SPEAKER

"The Phase Guides are incredibly creative, well researched, and filled with inspirational actions for everyday life. Each age-specific guide is catalytic for equipping parents to lead and love their kids as they grow up. I'm blown away and deeply encouraged by the content and by its creators. I highly recommend Phase resources for all parents, teachers, and influencers of children. This is the stuff that challenges us and changes our world. Get them. Read them. And use them!"

DANIELLE STRICKLAND
OFFICER WITH THE SALVATION ARMY, AUTHOR, SPEAKER, MOTHER OF TWO

"It's true that parenting is one of life's greatest joys but it is not without its challenges. If we're honest, parenting can sometimes feel like trying to choreograph a dance to an ever-changing beat. It can be clumsy and riddled with well-meaning missteps. If parenting is a dance, this Parenting Guide is a skilled instructor refining your technique and helping you move gracefully to a steady beat. For those of us who love to plan ahead, this guide will help you anticipate what's to come so you can be poised and ready to embrace the moments you want to enjoy."

TINA NAIDOO
MSSW, LCSW EXECUTIVE DIRECTOR, THE POTTER'S HOUSE OF DALLAS, INC.

PARENTING YOUR TENTH GRADER

A GUIDE TO MAKING THE MOST OF THE "WHY NOT?" PHASE

KRISTEN IVY AND REGGIE JOINER

PARENTING YOUR TENTH GRADER
A GUIDE TO MAKING THE MOST OF THE
"WHY NOT?" PHASE

Published by Orange, a division of The reThink Group, Inc.,
5870 Charlotte Lane, Suite 300,
Cumming, GA 30040 U.S.A.

©2017 Kristen Ivy and Reggie Joiner
Authors: Kristen Ivy and Reggie Joiner
Lead Editor: Karen Wilson
Editing Team: Melanie Williams, Hannah Crosby, Sherry Surratt

Art Direction: Ryan Boon and Hannah Crosby
Book Design: FiveStone and Sharon van Rossum

Printed in the United States of America
First Edition 2017
1 2 3 4 5 6 7 8 9 10

Special thanks to:

Jim Burns, Ph.D for guidance and consultation
on having conversations about sexual integrity

Jon Acuff for guidance and consultation on having
conversations about technological responsibility

Jean Sumner, MD for guidance and consultation
on having conversations about healthy habits

Every educator, counselor, community leader, and
researcher who invested in the Phase Project

TABLE OF CONTENTS

HOW TO USE THIS ~~BOOK~~ ~~JOURNAL~~ GUIDE

The guide you hold in your hand doesn't have very many words, but it does have a lot of ideas. Some of these ideas come from thousands of hours of research. Others come from parents, educators, and volunteers who spend every day with kids the same age as yours. This guide won't tell you everything about your kid, but it will tell you a few things about kids at this age.

The best way to use this guide is to take what these pages tell you about tenth graders and combine it with what you know is true about *your* tenth grader.

Let's sum it up:

THINGS ABOUT TENTH GRADERS +
THOUGHTS ABOUT *YOUR* TENTH GRADER =
YOUR GUIDE TO THE NEXT 52 WEEKS OF PARENTING

After each idea in this guide, there are pages with a few questions designed to prompt you to think about your kid, your family, and yourself as a parent. The only guarantee we give to parents who use this guide is this: You will mess up some things as a parent this year. Actually, that's a guarantee to every parent, regardless. But you, you picked up this book! You want to be a better parent. And that's what we hope this guide will do: help you parent your tenth grader just a little better, simply because you paused to consider a few ideas that can help you make the most of this phase.

THE TENTH GRADE PHASE

"The world is my oyster!"

I'm fairly certain Shakespeare was around the age of fifteen when he first wrote this phrase. I haven't fact-checked that tidbit of trivia, but it makes a lot of sense to me. It's a phrase to describe the feeling of someone who's young, healthy, has no commitments, and is free to do exactly as they want. So, basically, that's every tenth grader ever.

Sophomores are in the best phase of their lives. They have new levels of independence, freedom, and mobility. They're solidly assimilated into the social culture of high school. And yet, they have comparatively little responsibility for their financial needs, serious concerns over academic achievement, or anxieties regarding the future.

Tenth graders live in the here-and-now. They see the world as new, fresh, full of possibilities, and brimming with opportunities. They feel they are ready for every experience life has to offer. Why not? The world is their oyster.

As exciting as that may sound, many parents living with a teenager in this phase may use a different oyster metaphor to describe it—that it's like being forced to eat a *raw* one. I'm not a big fan of eating raw oysters. Sure, I realize some people *love* them—but I cannot get my brain (or tongue) around the concept of slurping down something that looks like a gigantic phlegm ball in a shell.

For some of us who have parented fifteen-year-olds, the Tenth Grade Phase may seem like nothing more than the "Really-Bad-Idea Phase." Because sophomores see the world as their oyster, they often move full-speed ahead, fueled by eager "Why nots?" I know. I've parented through it . . . three times.

The risks and dangers of their fearlessness often collide into the exploration of the "Big Ds" of drinking, drugs, dating, and driving. That makes for some pretty valid reasons why parents may find this oyster unpalatable. But resist the temptation to overly-focus on the negative—the risks, the dangers, and the absolutely crazy behaviors of your sophomore. Why? Because when you allow your fear to become your focus, you cut yourself off from sharing in the sheer *joy of life* your tenth grader is experiencing.

You have tremendous opportunity this year to shape the life of a budding adult. But if you want to have influence, now is the time to shift your parenting to become a coach. Just remember, athletes play the game and coaches coach. Your sophomore doesn't need (or want) you to live life for them, making their "in-game" decisions. But they absolutely need you to be "all-in" in terms of your commitment to being a great coach!

So this year, set healthy behavioral expectations and consequences. Offer plenty of space for them to make their own age-appropriate decisions. Be *consistently present* in their successes and failures. And most of all, become a liberal dispenser of affirmation, encouragement, grace, forgiveness, and love. When you take advantage of the divine opportunities for conversation and affirmation, this phase can be *your* best phase in parenting. The world is your sophomore's oyster. Help them find their pearl.

- DOUG FIELDS
EXECUTIVE DIRECTOR OF HOMEWORD'S CENTER FOR YOUTH AND FAMILY, CO-FOUNDER OF DOWNLOAD YOUTH MINISTRY, & AUTHOR OF MORE THAN 50 BOOKS

52 WEEKS

—

TO PARENT YOUR TENTH GRADER

WHEN YOU SEE
HOW MUCH

Time

YOU HAVE LEFT

—

YOU TEND TO DO

More

WITH THE TIME
YOU HAVE NOW.

THERE ARE APPROXIMATELY
936 WEEKS
FROM THE TIME A BABY IS BORN
UNTIL THEY GROW UP AND MOVE TO
WHATEVER IS NEXT.

On the day your kid starts tenth grade, you have 156 weeks remaining. Your tenth grader may act like your job as a parent is already over—unless they need some money. But your parenting isn't over yet. What happens this year can dramatically influence their future.

That's why every week counts. Of course, each week might not feel significant. There may be weeks this year when all you feel like you accomplished was researching ways to control your anxiety about all the things you no longer control. That's okay.

Take a deep breath.
You don't have to get everything done this week.

But what happens in your teenager's life week after week, for the next three years, adds up. So, it might be a good idea to put a number to your weeks.

MEASURE IT OUT.

Write down the number of weeks you have left with your tenth grader before they potentially graduate high school.

HINT: If you want a little help counting it out, you can download the free Parent Cue app on all mobile platforms.

_____

_____

_____

_____

CREATE A VISUAL COUNTDOWN.

 Find a jar and fill it with one marble for each week you have remaining with your tenth grader. Then remove one marble every week as a reminder to make the most of your time.

Where can you place your visual countdown so you will see it frequently?

_____

_____

_____

_____

_____

Which day of the week is best for you to remove a marble?

_____

_____

_____

Is there anything you want to do each week as you remove a marble? *(Examples: say a prayer, send an encouraging text, retell one favorite memory from this past week)*

_____

_____

_____

_____

_____

_____

_____

_____

_____

_____

_____

_____

EVERY PHASE IS A

TIMEFRAME

IN A KID'S LIFE

WHEN YOU CAN

LEVERAGE

DISTINCTIVE

OPPORTUNITIES

TO INFLUENCE

THEIR

future.

YOU ONLY HAVE
52 WEEKS
WITH YOUR TENTH GRADER

while they are still in tenth grade.

Then they will be in eleventh grade,

and you will never know them as a tenth grader again.

Or, to say it another way:

Before you know it, your teenager will . . .

drive themselves to school.

watch a rated R movie in the theater.

legally donate blood to the Red Cross.

That's not to stress you out.

It's to remind you of the potential of this phase.

Before tenth grade is finished, there are some distinctive opportunities you don't want to miss. So, as you count down the next 52 weeks with your tenth grader, pay attention to what makes these weeks uniquely different from the time you've already spent together and the weeks you will have when they move to the next phase.

Time travel for a minute. Remember what it was like to be in tenth grade. What are the best things your parents did for you during that phase of your life? What do you want to try to do differently than your parents?

_____

_____

_____

_____

_____

_____

_____

_____

_____

_____

_____

_____

_____

_____

_____

_____

_____

What do you think is going to be different about your tenth grader's sophomore year than *your* sophomore year?

_____

_____

_____

_____

_____

_____

_____

_____

_____

_____

_____

_____

_____

_____

_____

_____

_____

_____

_____

_____

_____

What are some things you have noticed about your tenth grader in this phase that you really enjoy?

_____
_____
_____
_____
_____
_____
_____
_____
_____
_____
_____
_____
_____
_____
_____
_____
_____
_____
_____

What is something new you're learning as a parent during this phase?

_____

_____

_____

_____

_____

_____

_____

_____

_____

_____

_____

_____

_____

_____

_____

_____

_____

_____

_____

_____

TENTH GRADE

—

THE PHASE WHEN
EVERYONE ELSE CAN . . .
NOBODY ELSE HAS TO . . .
AND YOUR RESOLUTE
TEEN WILL PUSH YOU TO
ANSWER,

"Why not?"

ANTICIPATE NEW INDEPENDENCE.

Sweet Sixteen means sweet freedom. Whether this is getting a driver's license, using public transportation, or hopping in an Uber, your teenager may no longer depend on you for transportation. This year, you may constantly question just how much is too much freedom.

EXPECT SOME FRESH SKEPTICISM.

With newfound freedom comes greater life experience. That really life-shattering bad thing you warned them about? They know someone who survived it. The standards you held up for them in the past? They may come to realize you haven't always lived by them. So, get ready for them to challenge you on . . . well, just about everything.

KEEP FIGHTING FOR THEIR HEART.

A sophomore still needs boundaries, but unless the boundaries make sense in light of their personal (and changing) beliefs, they won't stay within them. Just remember, when you "debate" (loudly) boundaries with a sophomore, stay in the present. They aren't challenging what you both want ten years from now, they just need you to understand what they need right now.

THIS
YEAR
YOUR
TENTH
GRADER
IS
changing.

PHYSICALLY

- Has difficulty falling asleep before 11pm (it's biological)

- Needs nine hours of sleep and one hour of exercise per day

- Girls have likely reached adult height and body development

- Guys may experience voice changes, weird dreams, and increased acne

MENTALLY

- Increasingly able to focus, recall, and organize information

- Keenly aware of global issues and may be critical of the adult world

- Highly self-aware; may occasionally think, "Everybody's watching me."

- Wired for risk-taking and sensational experiences

- Tends to be curious, inquisitive, and drawn toward the supernatural

SOCIALLY

- Increased interest in sexual expression; and dating may become more "committed"

- Increased susceptibility to date violence and rape (peaks at 16 years)

- May experience depression; highest year for teen suicide

- Desires responsibilities that increase freedom

EMOTIONALLY

- Feels empowered through choices rather than rules

- Responds well to specific praise

- Becoming aware of their personal tendencies and patterns

- Seeks experiences that create intense feelings and emotions

- May enjoy sharing ideas with adults who will listen

27

What are some changes you are noticing in your tenth grader?

_____

_____

_____

_____

_____

_____

_____

You may disagree with some of the characteristics we've shared about tenth graders. That's because every tenth grader is unique. What makes your tenth grader different from tenth graders in general?

_____

_____

_____

_____

_____

_____

_____

_____

What impresses you about your tenth grader?

Mark this page. Some weeks it may be easy to focus only on what your tenth grader does wrong, so try to catch them doing something right. Write it down here. If you want to be really thorough, there are about 52 blank lines.

_____

_____

_____

_____

_____

_____

_____

_____

_____

_____

_____

_____

_____

_____

_____

_____

_____

_____

_____

_____

_____

_____

_____

_____

_____

_____

_____

_____

_____

_____

_____

_____

_____

_____

_____

_____

_____

_____

_____

_____

_____

_____

SIX THINGS

—

EVERY KID NEEDS

YOUR KID NEEDS **6** THINGS OVER TIME

LOVE

WORDS

WORK

PEOPLE

STORIES

FUN

OVER THE NEXT 156 WEEKS, YOUR TENTH GRADER WILL NEED MANY THINGS:

Some of the things your teenager needs will change over the next 156 weeks, but there are six things every kid needs at every phase. In fact, these things may be the most important things you give your high schooler (even more important than money—but they will probably ask you for money more often).

EVERY KID, AT EVERY PHASE, NEEDS . . .

♡ LOVE
to give them a
sense of WORTH.

📖 STORIES
to give them a bigger
PERSPECTIVE.

🏋 WORK
to give them
PURPOSE.

♟ FUN
to give them
CONNECTION.

👥 PEOPLE
to give them
BELONGING.

💬 WORDS
to give them
DIRECTION.

The next few pages are designed to help you think about how you will give your teenager these six things, right now, while they are in tenth grade.

EVERY KID

NEEDS

love

OVER TIME

—

TO GIVE THEM

A SENSE OF

worth.

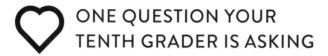

ONE QUESTION YOUR TENTH GRADER IS ASKING

Your tenth grader feels comfortable navigating the hallways of high school, and they are ready for more. Tenth graders are expanding their life experience. They will push the limits. They might even rebel a little—even though you never did.

Your tenth grader is asking one major question:

"WHY SHOULD I BELIEVE?"

Or, you might rephrase that, "Why should I believe *you*?" But even in the times when tensions are high, remember—there are 156 weeks. And this is an important year. The best way to love your tenth grader is to do one thing:

MOBILIZE their potential.

Your tenth grader will feel most loved when they are around people who help them discover their voice, their passion, and their values. You mobilize their potential when you communicate . . .

"I'm listening, help me understand,"

"I trust you, help me trust you more,"

and "You can always tell me, because I love you no matter what."

Mobilizing your sophomore's potential requires paying attention to what they like. What does your tenth grader seem to enjoy the most right now? *(If you don't know, it's okay to ask them.)*

_____

_____

_____

_____

_____

_____

_____

_____

_____

_____

_____

_____

_____

_____

_____

_____

_____

_____

Mobilizing your tenth grader toward future freedom also
requires boundaries. What are the most important boundaries
for your tenth grader?

_____

_____

_____

_____

_____

_____

_____

_____

_____

_____

_____

_____

_____

_____

_____

_____

_____

_____

_____

What are the consequences when your tenth grader breaks a rule? *(Consider deciding on rules and consequences together. Talk about ways they can earn future freedom as they build trust.)*

As you know, parenting a teenager can be tough. It's impossible to love your tenth grader well if you are running on empty. What can you do to refuel each week so you are able to give your tenth grader the love they need?

_____

_____

_____

_____

_____

_____

_____

_____

_____

_____

_____

_____

_____

_____

_____

_____

_____

_____

_____

_____

BOOKS YOUR TENTH GRADER MIGHT BE READING

I KNOW WHY THE CAGED BIRD SINGS
by Maya Angelou

PRIDE AND PREJUDICE
by Jane Austen

A LONG WAY GONE
by Ishmael Beah

THE PERKS OF BEING A WALLFLOWER
by Stephen Chbosky

THE HOUSE ON MANGO STREET
by Sandra Cisneros

THE HUNT FOR RED OCTOBER
by Tom Clancy

HARD TIMES
by Charles Dickens

LORD OF THE FLIES
by William Golding

LOOKING FOR ALASKA
by John Green

UNBROKEN
by Laura Hillenbrand

LES MISERABLES
by Victor Hugo

THE BOY WHO HARNESSED THE WIND
by William Kamkwamba and Bryan Mealer

A SEPARATE PEACE
by John Knowles

THE COLOR OF WATER
by James McBride

1984
by George Orwell

THE SCARLET PIMPERNEL
by Baroness Orczy

OF MICE AND MEN
by John Steinbeck

WILD
by Cheryl Strayed

UP FROM SLAVERY
by Booker T. Washington

THE BOOK THIEF
by Marcus Zusak

Share a story. Whether it's a book, play, TV series, or movie, what are some stories that engage your sophomore?

_____

_____

_____

_____

_____

_____

_____

_____

_____

_____

_____

_____

_____

_____

_____

_____

_____

_____

_____

What might happen to your relationship when you watch or
read the same story together?

Tell a story. As you watch your tenth grader live out their story, how can you act like a narrator to help them interpret who they are and what's happening? (*Example: "You seem really happy when you get to build something with your hands."*)

_____

_____

_____

_____

_____

_____

_____

_____

_____

_____

_____

_____

_____

_____

_____

_____

_____

_____

Live a story. When a tenth grader serves others, they broaden their perspective by learning about someone else's story. Is there somewhere your tenth grader would enjoy serving on a regular basis?

_____

_____

_____

_____

_____

_____

_____

_____

_____

_____

_____

_____

_____

_____

_____

_____

_____

_____

EVERY KID

NEEDS

work

OVER TIME

—

TO GIVE

THEM

purpose.

WORK YOUR TENTH GRADER CAN DO

DO HOMEWORK

BABYSIT

MANAGE A PERSONAL CALENDAR

PREPARE A FAMILY MEAL

SORT, WASH, FOLD, AND PUT AWAY LAUNDRY

CHECK OIL AND TIRE PRESSURE IN THE CAR
(and add air as needed)

LEARN TO JUMP START A CAR

DO SIMPLE HOME REPAIRS
(fix a leak or the hinge on a cabinet)

GET A FIRST JOB
(grocery bagger, coach or referee, fast food server)

HELP PAY A PERSONAL BILL
(car insurance, phone bill)

FILL OUT A W-4, READ A PAY STUB, AND LEARN ABOUT TAXES

VOLUNTEER WITH KIDS OR MIDDLE SCHOOLERS

What are some ways your tenth grader already shows responsibility at home, at school, and in-between?

_____

_____

_____

_____

_____

_____

_____

_____

_____

_____

_____

_____

_____

_____

_____

_____

_____

_____

_____

How can you collaborate with your sophomore to agree on which of their responsibilities matter most for your family and their future?

_____

_____

_____

_____

_____

_____

_____

_____

_____

_____

_____

_____

_____

_____

_____

_____

_____

Some days might be easier than others to motivate your tenth grader. What are some strategies you could employ to keep your tenth grader motivated?

What are things you (and your tenth grader) hope they will be able to do independently next year? How are you helping them develop those skills now?

WAYS TO HAVE FUN
WITH YOUR TENTH GRADER

WATCH A MOVIE

ATTEND A SPORTING EVENT

GO TO A CONCERT

WORK OUT TOGETHER

PLAY MUSIC TOGETHER

BUILD SOMETHING

COOK SOMETHING

GO ON A RUN

GO ON A HIKE

GO SHOPPING

SHOOT SOME HOOPS

WORK ON CAR REPAIRS

GET A MANICURE

WATCH A TV SERIES

GO TO A PLAY

GO FISHING

GO BOWLING

PLAY LASER TAG

HAVE A RESTAURANT THAT'S "YOURS"

TRY A NEW RESTAURANT OR FOOD TRUCK

PLANT A GARDEN

PLAY A BOARD GAME

PLAY A VIDEO GAME

PLAY CARDS

PLAY A GAME ON A PHONE APP

LAUNCH MODEL ROCKETS

LEARN TO DANCE

GO TO THE LAKE

RIDE A ROLLER COASTER

GO OUT FOR COFFEE

GO OUT FOR ICE CREAM

GO SEE A COMEDIAN

Whatever you do together for fun, try to offer suggestions based on what they enjoy—even at the expense of what you might enjoy a little more.

What are some activities your tenth grader enjoys that you could do as a family (*and maybe sometimes include their friends*)?

_____

_____

_____

_____

_____

_____

_____

_____

_____

_____

_____

_____

_____

_____

_____

_____

_____

_____

What are some activities your tenth grader enjoys that you could occasionally do together, one-on-one?

_____

_____

_____

_____

_____

_____

_____

_____

When are the best times of the day, or week, for you to set aside to just have fun with your tenth grader?

_____

_____

_____

_____

_____

_____

_____

Some days are *extra* fun days. What are some ways you want to celebrate the special days coming up this year?

NEXT BIRTHDAY

HOLIDAYS

Consider celebrating a few random holidays: the first/last day of school, the day they get a driver's license or learner's permit, PSAT testing day, homecoming.

ADULTS WHO MIGHT INFLUENCE YOUR TENTH GRADER

PARENTS

COMMUNITY LEADERS

CHURCH LEADERS

GRANDPARENTS

FRIENDS' PARENTS

COACHES

CLUB SPONSORS

HIGH SCHOOL TEACHERS

BOSS OR CO-WORKERS
(at an after-school job)

As great as you are *(and you're clearly an awesome parent)* you aren't the only adult influence your tenth grader needs. List at least five adults who have the potential to positively influence your tenth grader.

_____

_____

_____

_____

_____

_____

_____

_____

_____

_____

_____

_____

_____

_____

_____

_____

_____

What would be good information for these people to know if they want to help or support your tenth grader this year?

_____

_____

_____

_____

_____

_____

_____

_____

_____

_____

_____

_____

_____

_____

_____

_____

_____

_____

_____

_____

_____

_____

What are some upcoming events in your tenth grader's life that you could invite one or more of these adults to attend?

_____

_____

_____

_____

_____

_____

_____

_____

_____

_____

_____

_____

_____

_____

_____

_____

_____

_____

_____

What are a few ways you could show these adults appreciation for the significant role they play in your kid's life?

_____

_____

_____

_____

_____

_____

_____

_____

_____

_____

_____

_____

_____

_____

_____

_____

_____

_____

_____

WORDS YOUR TENTH GRADER NEEDS TO HEAR

GOOD MORNING!

I LOVE YOU

TELL ME MORE

HOW CAN I HELP?

WHAT DO YOU THINK?

I'M SORRY THAT I . . .

YOU IMPRESSED ME WHEN YOU . . .

YOU HAVE A UNIQUE WAY OF . . .

WANT A HUG?

I LIKE YOU

YOU ARE BEAUTIFUL / HANDSOME

THANK YOU FOR SPENDING TIME WITH US.

GOOD NIGHT!

ME TOO

I LIKE HAVING YOU HOME

What are some ways you can share personal and specific encouragement with your tenth grader?

Hint: You might start with the things that impress you about your tenth grader from page 29.

_____

_____

_____

_____

_____

_____

_____

_____

_____

_____

_____

_____

_____

_____

_____

_____

_____

You might be impressed by the words that inspire your tenth grader. How can you encourage your tenth grader to share a quote, song lyric, Scripture, or thought that inspired them?

_____

_____

_____

_____

_____

_____

_____

_____

_____

_____

_____

_____

_____

_____

_____

_____

_____

_____

_____

What are some quotes, lyrics, Scriptures, or inspirational thoughts you want to share with your tenth grader? Make it a habit to regularly text or send encouraging thoughts their way.

FOUR
CONVERSATIONS

—

TO HAVE IN THIS
PHASE

WHEN YOU KNOW
WHERE YOU WANT
TO GO,

AND YOU KNOW
WHERE YOU ARE
NOW,

YOU CAN ALWAYS
DO SOMETHING

TO MOVE IN A
BETTER DIRECTION.

OVER THE NEXT 156 WEEKS, IT MAY BE HARD TO FIND TIME FOR CONVERSATIONS. WHEN YOU *DO* GET A FEW MINUTES TO TALK, IT CAN BE HARD TO KNOW WHAT TO SAY FIRST.

You want to ask about tomorrow's exam.

They want to ask for gas money.

But, in the middle of everything that's urgent, don't forget to have a few important conversations along the way as well.

WHAT YOU SAY ABOUT . . . | **MAY IMPACT YOUR TENTH GRADER'S FUTURE EVEN MORE THAN CHEMISTRY MIDTERMS.**

Health

Sex

Technology

or Faith

The next pages are about the conversations that matter most. On the left page is a destination—what you might want to be true in your kid's life 156 weeks from now. On the right page is a goal for conversations with your tenth grader this year, and a few suggestions about what you might want to say.

Healthy habits

LEARNING TO
STRENGTHEN
MY BODY THROUGH
EXERCISE, NUTRITION,
AND SELF-ADVOCACY

THIS YEAR YOU WILL

ENCOURAGE A HEALTHY LIFESTYLE

SO THEY WILL SHARPEN THEIR PERSONAL AWARENESS AND BALANCE DIET AND EXERCISE.

Maintain a good relationship with your pediatrician, and schedule a physical at least once per year. You can also encourage your tenth grader to develop healthy habits with a few simple words.

SAY THINGS LIKE . . .

"SHAVE IN THE SAME DIRECTION THE HAIR GROWS."
(Teach guys how to shave when you start to see facial hair.)

"FAST WEIGHT LOSS ISN'T REALLY HEALTHY."
(Talk about healthy ways to diet and lose weight.)

"WOULD YOU BE INTERESTED IN SEEING A COUNSELOR TO TALK ABOUT THAT?"
(Teenagers often need counseling for emotional support and coaching.)

HAVE YOU EVER TRIED TZATZIKI SAUCE?
(Try new foods together.)

"WOULD YOU LIKE TO GO ON A RUN WITH ME?"
(Stay active together.)

"YOU DON'T SEEM TO BE EATING AS MUCH AS YOU USED TO."
(Pay attention to sudden changes in weight, appetite, clothing, interests, and behaviors.)

What are some activities you can do with your tenth grader that require a little bit of exercise?

_____

_____

_____

_____

_____

_____

_____

_____

_____

_____

_____

_____

_____

_____

_____

_____

_____

_____

_____

_____

At some point, your kid will be responsible for selecting or preparing what they eat. How can you help them get ready for that reality by giving them opportunities to practice meal-planning, grocery shopping, and cooking?

_____

_____

_____

_____

_____

_____

_____

_____

_____

_____

_____

_____

_____

_____

_____

_____

_____

_____

_____

Do you have any specific concerns when it comes to your tenth grader's physical or mental health? Who will help you monitor and improve their health this year?

_____

_____

_____

_____

_____

_____

_____

_____

_____

_____

_____

_____

_____

_____

_____

_____

_____

_____

What are your own health goals for this year? How can you improve the habits in your own life?

_____

_____

_____

_____

_____

_____

_____

_____

_____

_____

_____

_____

_____

_____

_____

_____

_____

_____

_____

_____

Sexual
integrity

—

GUARDING MY
POTENTIAL FOR
INTIMACY THROUGH
APPROPRIATE
BOUNDARIES
AND MUTUAL
RESPECT

THIS YEAR YOU WILL

COACH THEM TOWARD HEALTHY RELATIONSHIPS

SO THEY WILL ESTABLISH PERSONAL BOUNDARIES AND PRACTICE MUTUAL RESPECT.

The tenth grade drive for personal experience influences the way many tenth graders experiment with dating and relationships. Like a good coach, pay close attention to the game. Be smart about how you guard your sophomore while still allowing them enough freedom to solidify personal boundaries.

SAY THINGS LIKE . . .

"THANK YOU FOR TALKING ABOUT THIS. CAN WE TALK ABOUT IT AGAIN ANOTHER TIME?"
(Always finish the conversation with room to pick it back up again later.)

"THANK YOU FOR TELLING ME."

"I'M SO GLAD YOU ASKED ME."

"HOW OFTEN DO YOU STILL TALK WITH YOUR OTHER FRIENDS?"
(If your tenth grader is dating, ask questions to help them think objectively about the relationship.)

WHAT DO YOU THINK ABOUT THAT?
(Give them a safe place to process values with you.)

"HOW DO THEY MAKE YOU FEEL ABOUT YOURSELF?"

"IF YOU EVER FEEL LIKE SOMEONE IS WANTING YOU TO DO SOMETHING YOU DON'T WANT TO DO, YOU COULD ALWAYS SAY . . . "
(Help them script responses to difficult situations)

What guardrails do you have in place to help protect your sophomore when it comes to dating and sexuality?

_____

_____

_____

_____

_____

_____

_____

_____

_____

_____

_____

_____

_____

_____

_____

_____

_____

_____

_____

_____

_____

Who, besides you, is influencing your sophomore's values about
dating and sexuality?

_____

_____

_____

_____

_____

_____

_____

_____

_____

_____

_____

_____

_____

_____

_____

_____

_____

_____

_____

_____

_____

Fifty percent of those who report having coerced someone else into sexual activity say they first forced someone when they were sixteen years old. How can you guide your tenth grader to know how to get out of potentially dangerous situations?

_____

_____

_____

_____

_____

_____

_____

_____

_____

_____

_____

_____

_____

_____

_____

_____

_____

Plan ahead. Write down two or three things you want to say to your kid if you were to discover something you hadn't expected when it comes to their sexuality. *(It's okay to pray you never have to say these things.)*

_____

_____

_____

_____

_____

_____

_____

_____

_____

_____

_____

_____

_____

_____

_____

_____

_____

Technological responsibility

—

LEVERAGING THE POTENTIAL OF ONLINE EXPERIENCES TO ENHANCE MY OFFLINE COMMUNITY AND SUCCESS

THIS YEAR YOU WILL
EXPAND THEIR POTENTIAL
SO THEY WILL ESTABLISH PERSONAL BOUNDARIES AND LEVERAGE ONLINE OPPORTUNITIES.

Your tenth grader is online with 3.2 billion other people, or about 40% of the world's current population. That's a lot of potential. Potential to learn. Potential to share. Potential to collaborate for a cause. Stay actively engaged in all the ways your tenth grader explores the potential that is now literally at their fingertips.

SAY THINGS LIKE . . .

"I LOVE THAT KICKSTARTER YOU SHARED."

"I'M SO IMPRESSED WITH YOUR ETSY SHOP."

"HOW DO YOU SET UP A YOUTUBE CHANNEL?"

"LET'S SPLIT THE BILL 80/20."
(Consider sharing the bill.)

YOU CANNOT USE YOUR PHONE TO TEXT OR CALL WHILE DRIVING.
(Have clear expectations for cell phones and driving.)

"HELP ME UNDERSTAND WHY."
(Listen to their reasoning, and look for common ground.)

What are some ways you've seen your tenth grader use technology to do something good?

_____

_____

_____

_____

_____

_____

_____

_____

_____

_____

_____

_____

_____

_____

_____

_____

_____

_____

_____

What are your concerns about your tenth grader's engagement with digital devices? What rules do you have to help monitor and guard their engagement?

_____

_____

_____

_____

_____

_____

_____

_____

_____

_____

_____

_____

_____

_____

_____

_____

_____

_____

_____

When you aren't sure what to do about an issue related to parenting and technology, who can you go to for advice?

_____

_____

_____

_____

_____

_____

_____

_____

_____

_____

_____

_____

_____

_____

_____

_____

_____

_____

_____

_____

What are your own personal values and disciplines when it comes to leveraging technology? Are there ways you want to improve your own savvy, skill, or responsibility in this area?

_____

_____

_____

_____

_____

_____

_____

_____

_____

_____

_____

_____

_____

_____

_____

_____

_____

_____

_____

Authentic faith

—

TRUSTING JESUS IN A WAY THAT TRANSFORMS HOW I LOVE GOD, MYSELF, AND THE REST OF THE WORLD

THIS YEAR YOU WILL

FUEL PASSION

SO THEY WILL KEEP PURSUING AUTHENTIC FAITH AND DISCOVER A PERSONAL MISSION.

In this phase when your tenth grader is asking, "Why should I believe?" the best thing you can give them is a consistent faith community where they can process their doubts and strengthen their relationship with God. Stay engaged in their personal faith journey by having conversations at home.

SAY THINGS LIKE . . .

> **ARE THERE WAYS YOU WOULD WANT TO SERVE IN OUR CHURCH OR COMMUNITY?**

"HOW CAN I PRAY FOR YOU TODAY / THIS WEEK?"

"WHEN DO YOU FEEL CLOSEST TO GOD?"

"WHAT'S SOMETHING YOU FEEL LIKE GOD IS TEACHING YOU RIGHT NOW?"

"LATELY I'M FINDING I CONNECT BEST WITH GOD WHEN I'M . . . "

"THERE'S NOTHING YOU WILL EVER DO THAT COULD MAKE GOD STOP LOVING YOU."

"I DON'T KNOW."

"THAT'S A GOOD QUESTION. I'M NOT SURE I WILL EVER KNOW THE FULL ANSWER, BUT I BELIEVE . . . "
(Let them know it's okay to talk about hard questions.)

"WHEN YOU TOLD ME ABOUT . . . IT MADE ME THINK OF A VERSE IN PROVERBS."
(Share Bible verses that relate to their present circumstances.)

What are some ways you can help deepen your sophomore's connection with friends and adult leaders who follow Jesus?

_____

_____

_____

_____

_____

_____

_____

_____

_____

_____

_____

_____

_____

_____

_____

_____

_____

_____

Has your sophomore expressed questions or doubts about faith? How do you hope to respond if your sophomore challenges what your family believes?

_____

_____

_____

_____

_____

_____

_____

_____

_____

_____

_____

_____

_____

_____

_____

_____

_____

_____

_____

What are some retreats, youth camps, or mission trip opportunities provided by your church or a local youth ministry? Which ones seem most appealing to your tenth grader?

_____

_____

_____

_____

_____

_____

_____

_____

_____

_____

_____

_____

_____

_____

_____

_____

_____

_____

_____

What service opportunities are available for high schoolers at your church? What would it take for you to help them participate?

_____

_____

_____

_____

_____

_____

_____

_____

_____

_____

_____

_____

_____

_____

_____

_____

_____

THE

rhythm

OF YOUR

WEEK

—

WILL SHAPE

THE VALUES

IN YOUR

home.

NOW THAT YOU HAVE FILLED THIS BOOK WITH IDEAS, IT MAY SEEM AS IF YOU WILL NEVER HAVE TIME TO GET IT ALL DONE.

Actually, you have *156 weeks.*

And every week has potential.

The secret to making the most of this phase is to find time to spend together—even if it's only a couple hours each week. You may have less quality time together, but look for opportunities during three consistent times (and one that's less predictable).

Instill purpose by starting the day with encouraging words.

Connect regularly by scheduling time to eat together (even if it's once a week).

Interpret life when they occasionally open up at the end of the day. (Stay consistently available—just in case.)

Strengthen your relationship by adjusting your plans to show up whenever they need you.

How are you adjusting to a new rhythm in this phase?

What are some of your favorite traditions with your tenth grader?

_____

_____

_____

_____

_____

_____

_____

_____

_____

_____

_____

_____

_____

_____

_____

_____

_____

_____

_____

_____

_____

_____

Write down any other thoughts or questions about parenting your tenth grader.

_____

_____

_____

_____

_____

_____

_____

_____

_____

_____

_____

_____

_____

_____

_____

_____

_____

_____

_____

_____

_____

_____

_____

_____

_____

_____

_____

_____

_____

_____

_____

_____

_____

_____

_____

_____

_____

_____

_____

_____

_____

_____

YOU HAVE

APPROXIMATELY

156 WEEKS.

IT'S JUST
A PHASE
SO DON'T
MISS IT.

ABOUT THE AUTHORS

KRISTEN IVY @kristen_ivy

Kristen Ivy is executive director of the Phase Project. She and her husband, Matt, are in the preschool and elementary phases with three kids: Sawyer, Hensley, and Raleigh.

Kristen earned her Bachelors of Education from Baylor University in 2004 and received a Master of Divinity from Mercer University in 2009. She worked in the public school system as a high school biology and English teacher, where she learned firsthand the importance of influencing the next generation.

Kristen is also the President at Orange and has played an integral role in the development of the elementary, middle school, and high school curriculum and has shared her experiences at speaking events across the country. She is the co-author of *Playing for Keeps*, *Creating a Lead Small Culture*, *It's Just a Phase*, and *Don't Miss It*.

REGGIE JOINER @reggiejoiner

Reggie Joiner is founder and CEO of the reThink Group and co-founder of the Phase Project. He and his wife, Debbie, have reared four kids into adulthood. They now also have two grandchildren.

The reThink Group (also known as Orange) is a non-profit organization whose purpose is to influence those who influence the next generation. Orange provides resources and training for churches and organizations that create environments for parents, kids, and teenagers.

Before starting the reThink Group in 2006, Reggie was one of the founders of North Point Community Church. During his 11 years with Andy Stanley, Reggie was the executive director of family ministry, where he developed a new concept for relevant ministry to children, teenagers, and married adults. Reggie has authored and co-authored more than 10 books including: *Think Orange, Seven Practices of Effective Ministry, Parenting Beyond Your Capacity, Playing for Keeps, Lead Small, Creating a Lead Small Culture*, and his latest, *A New Kind of Leader* and *Don't Miss It.*

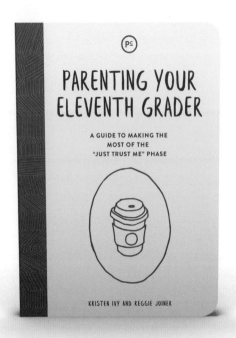

MAKE THE MOST OF EVERY PHASE IN YOUR CHILD'S LIFE

The guide in your hand is one of an eighteen-part series.

So, unless you've figured out a way to freeze time and keep your tenth grader from turning into a eleventh grader, you might want to check out the next guide in this set.

Designed in partnership with Parent Cue, each guide will help you rediscover . . .

what's changing about your kid,
the 6 things your kid needs most,
and 4 conversations to have each year.